HAL•LEONARD
INSTRUMENTAL
PLAY-ALONG

AUDIO
ACCESS
INCLUDED

PLAYBACK+
Speed • Pitch • Balance • Loop

CLARINET

12 POP HITS

Audio Arrangements by Peter Deneff

To access audio visit:
www.halleonard.com/mylibrary

Enter Code
7378-1908-7484-7989

ISBN 978-1-5400-2047-5

HAL•LEONARD®

7777 W. BLUEMOUND RD. P.O. BOX 13819 MILWAUKEE, WI 53213

Visit Hal Leonard Online at
www.halleonard.com

BELIEVER

Clarinet

Words and Music by DAN REYNOLDS,
WAYNE SERMON, BEN McKEE, DANIEL PLATZMAN,
JUSTIN TRANTOR, MATTIAS LARSSON and ROBIN FREDRICKSSON

CAN'T STOP THE FEELING

from TROLLS

Clarinet

Words and Music by JUSTIN TIMBERLAKE,
MAX MARTIN and SHELLBACK

DESPACITO

CLARINET

Words and Music by LUIS FONSI,
ERIKA ENDER, JUSTIN BIEBER, JASON BOYD,
MARTY JAMES GARTON and RAMON AYALA

Moderately, in 2
Keyboard

IT AIN'T ME

Clarinet

Words and Music by ALI TAMPOSI,
SELENA GOMEZ, ANDREW WOTMAN,
KYRRE GORVELL-DAHLL and BRIAN LEE

LOOK WHAT YOU MADE ME DO

Clarinet

Words and Music by TAYLOR SWIFT,
JACK ANTONOFF, RICHARD FAIRBRASS,
FRED FAIRBRASS and ROB MANZOLI

MILLION REASONS

Clarinet

Words and Music by STEFANI GERMANOTTA,
MARK RONSON and HILLARY LINDSEY

PERFECT

CLARINET

Words and Music by
ED SHEERAN

SEND MY LOVE
(To Your New Lover)

Clarinet

Words and Music by ADELE ADKINS,
MAX MARTIN and SHELLBACK

SHAPE OF YOU

CLARINET

Words and Music by ED SHEERAN,
KEVIN BRIGGS, KANDI BURRUSS, TAMEKA COTTLE,
STEVE MAC and JOHNNY McDAID

Play 3 times

Play 3 times

SLOW HANDS

CLARINET

Words and Music by NIALL HORAN,
JOHN HENRY RYAN, ALEXANDER IZQUIERDO,
RUTH-ANNE CUNNINGHAM, TOBIAS JESSO JR.
and JULIAN BUNETTA

TOO GOOD AT GOODBYES

Clarinet

Words and Music by SAM SMITH,
TOR HERMANSEN, MIKKEL ERIKSEN
and JAMES NAPIER

WHAT ABOUT US

Clarinet

Words and Music by ALECIA MOORE,
STEVE MAC and JOHNNY McDAID